MICHAEL JACKSON

Vicky Shipton

CB019345

LEVEL 3

■SCHOLASTIC

Written by: Vicky Shipton

Publisher: Jacquie Bloese

Designer: drbamboo

Picture research: Emma Bree

Photo credits:

Cover: K. Djansezian/AP.

Pages 4 & 5: Bettmann, W. Maldonado/Corbis; Berliner Studio Inc, Sipa/Rex; A. Lambert/Getty Images; F. Bensch, HO/Reuters.

Page 6: S. Karpukhin/Reuters. **Page 8:** T. Arroy/Corbis.

Pages 10 & 11: M. Ochs/Getty Images; Bettmann/Corbis.

Page 13: Newspix/Rex. **Page 15:** Bettmann/Corbis.

Page 16: A. Messer/Rex. **Page 19:** Universal/EVT/Rex.

Page 21: London Features International.

Page 22: Sony, Mary Glasgow Magazines.

Page 24: Sony/Allstar. **Page 27:** NBCU Photobank/Rex.

Page 28: L. McLendon/AP. **Page 30:** AP/PA.

Pages 32 & 33: EVT/Rex; Sony.

Page 35: S. Kokin/Julien's Auctions/Rex.

Pages 36 & 37: WENN; All Action/PA. **Page 39:** Reuters.

Page 41: J. Paschal/London Features International.

Page 42: WENN. **Pages 44 & 45:** Sipa/Rex; DPA/PA.

Page 49: K. White/Corbis. **Page 51:** AP/PA.

Page 52: D. Hogan/Getty Images.

Page 54: K. Djansezian/Getty Images.

Pages 56 & 57: K. Mazur/Wireimage, F. Micelotta, A. Wong, T. Canham, M. Anzuoni/Getty Images; Twitter.

Pages 58 & 59: EVT, D. Hoffmann/Rex; Sony/Allstar.

Pages 60 & 61: AFP/Getty Images; EVT, Sipa, A. Michael, E. McCreight/Rex.

Published by Scholastic Ltd. 2009

Mary Glasgow Magazines (Scholastic Ltd.)
Euston House
24 Eversholt Street
London NW1 IDB

Printed in Singapore. Reprinted in 2010.

CONTENTS

MICHAEL JACKSON
1958-2009

Michael, age 12, with his brothers in The Jackson 5

Michael, 1983

Michael's mum, Katherine Jackson

Michael and his dad, Joe Jackson, 1994

Michael and first wife, Lisa Marie Presley, 1994

Michael and second wife, Debbie Rowe. Married, 15th November, 1996.

Family day in Berlin Zoo. Michael with two of his children, Prince Michael I and Paris.

PLACES

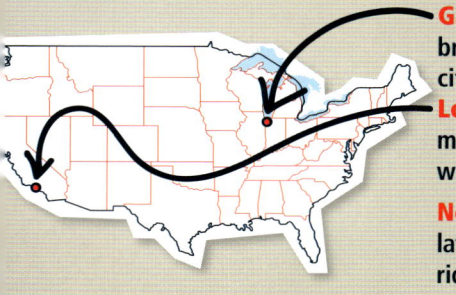

Gary, Indiana: Michael and his brothers were born in this poor city, near Chicago.

Los Angeles (LA): Michael moved to this city in California when he was eleven.

Neverland: Michael's home in later years in California. It had fair rides and lots of unusual animals.

MICHAEL JACKSON

THE KING OF POP IS DEAD

On the afternoon of the 25th June, 2009, Michael Jackson died of a heart attack in a hospital in Los Angeles. In less than an hour, the news was on websites all over the world. Was it really true? Millions of people visited Michael Jackson's pages on Facebook and Wikipedia. It was the same story everywhere: the 'King of Pop' was dead.

The traffic in Los Angeles stopped moving. The streets were full of the sound of Michael Jackson's music, as people played his hits from cars and shops.

Michael Jackson was the biggest star in the world. He sold more records and won more awards than any other singer. But he was famous for other reasons, too. Why did he change his appearance so much? Why did he sometimes seem to enjoy the company of children more than adults? Why didn't he perform on stage for so many years?

Who was Michael Jackson? Part of the answer lies in a small house near the city of Chicago . . . .

CHAPTER 1
AT HOME WITH THE JACKSONS

'Hey! Who did this? Tito? Jermaine? Jackie? Come here now!'

Joe Jackson was angry . . . and the Jackson children knew that one of them was in big trouble. Someone had gone into their father's room and played his guitar. Now it was broken.

That guitar was special to Joe Jackson. He worked long, hard hours in his job, but he had always had big dreams. He used to play the guitar in a band at local bars and clubs. The band had not succeeded and Joe's dreams disappeared.

Joe soon found out the truth. His son Tito was playing the guitar while Joe was at work. Tito's brothers, Jackie and Jermaine, were singing along with him. When he heard this, Joe hit Tito with his belt.

The boy was still crying when Joe came into his room.

'Let me see what you can do,' Joe said, giving the guitar to his son.

As Tito played and his two brothers sang, Joe saw a different future for the family. In his opinion, you were either one of life's winners or you were a loser. His own band had failed, but he was looking now at another chance for a better life. His children could form a band!

Born in 1958, Michael Jackson was the seventh of nine children. The Jacksons lived in a little house on Jackson Street in Gary, Indiana, a poor city near Chicago, full of factories and thousands of other small houses. Michael later described their home as 'no bigger than a garage'. (Their address later became famous in the song '2300 Jackson Street'.) All the boys slept in one of the two bedrooms; the family's three girls – Rebbie, LaToya and, later, Janet – slept on sofas in the living room.

As a child, Michael Jackson was very close to his mother, Katherine. Her religion and family were the most important things in life to her. Michael later said that she had taught him valuable lessons about love and kindness. He thought that his beautiful singing voice came from her, too. Michael's feelings for his father were very different. Like the rest of the children, he was afraid of Joseph Jackson. Michael was a shy, quiet child, and he often tried to avoid his father.

At first Michael was not part of Joe's big plan to make a band with his sons; he was still a small child. The young Michael watched as Joe made three of his brothers – Jackie, Tito and Jermaine – practise their music, before and after school. He didn't let them play with other children;

their whole world was the family and their band. Soon Michael's brother Marlon joined the band, too. At the age of four, Michael started singing along with Jermaine. Hearing the boy's strong, clear voice, Katherine knew that he was special. Now she had an idea: 'Why doesn't Michael join the group?' The Jackson 5 were born!

The boys practised hard together – Joe didn't allow anything else. 'He didn't make it fun,' Michael later remembered. Joe became the band's manager and started putting them into talent competitions. Every weekend he drove them to different cities to sing in clubs or competitions.

One thing became clear – although Michael was a quiet boy at home, he was a natural star in front of the microphone. Soon he, not Jermaine, was the band's main singer. Joe could see that Michael's talent was special. Sometimes he shouted at the other boys, 'Do it like Michael!'

Michael hated this. 'I didn't want to be the example,' he once said.

The Jackson 5 became more and more successful, and Joe found a local record company to sell their music. In 1968, the band recorded their first two songs. Neither was a hit, but now the band was playing bigger concerts around the country. Michael always studied the other singers carefully. When James Brown* was singing on TV, Michael watched all of his dance moves . Although he was young, Michael was serious about being the best.

In July 1968, the band went to Detroit* because Motown Records wanted to hear them. Joe knew that this was an

* James Brown was a famous African-American singer in the 1960s.
* Detroit is a city in America. The offices of Motown Records used to be here.

important meeting – Motown had produced some of the greatest ever records by African-American* musicians. The boys played for a group of the company's bosses. When they finished, the Motown people wrote down some notes, and didn't say very much. It was a scary moment – did Motown like The Jackson 5 or not?

The Jacksons had to wait for the answer. The head of Motown, Berry Gordy, had moved from Detroit to Los Angeles (LA). A film of the Jacksons' songs was sent to him. Three days later, a message from Gordy arrived – Motown wanted The Jackson 5! They were on their way!

In 1969, The Jackson 5 and their father moved to Los Angeles to chase their dream of success. The rest of the family stayed in their little house in Gary. In LA the boys lived with their father in cheap hotels, but to Michael the city was beautiful. He and his brothers still went to school, but they spent the rest of their time at work in Motown's LA studios.

* An 'African-American' is a black person who was born in the USA.

At last, Gordy decided that they were ready. He told the boys about his plans for three singles by The Jackson 5.

'They won't only be hits,' promised Gordy. 'They will be number one hits!'

He introduced the band to Diana Ross who was one of Motown's biggest stars. She offered to help the band, inviting lots of important people to a club to see them. The invitation said that the eight-year-old Michael Jackson would perform there. In fact Michael's real age was ten. Diana told a worried Michael that it was a better story for the press this way.

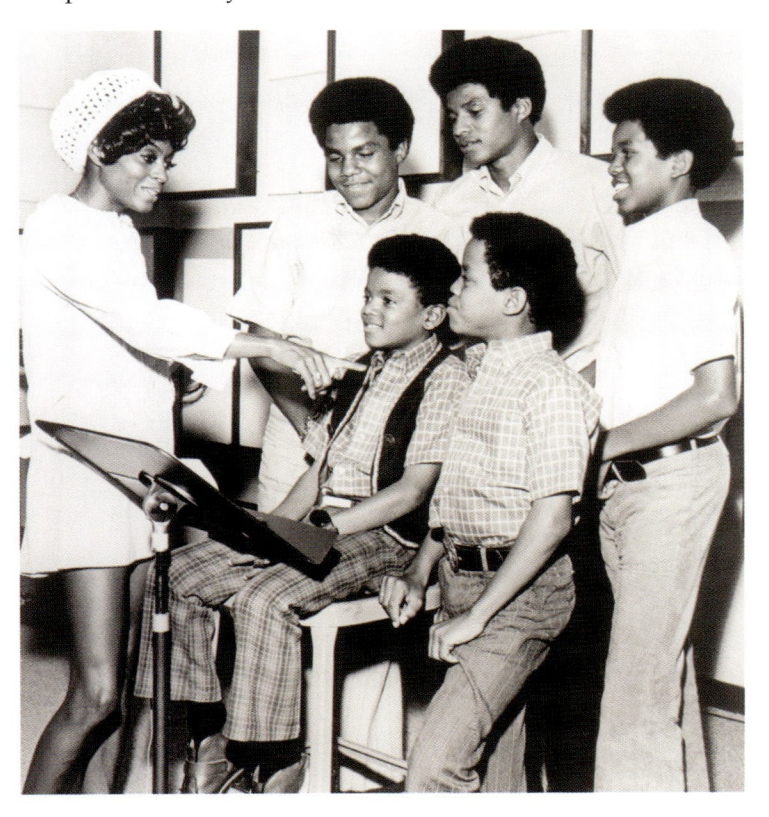

That night The Jackson 5 were a huge success. Dressed in green suits and gold shirts, they performed lots of popular Motown songs. After the concert, a reporter asked Michael his age. He replied that he was eight. He was already learning the rules of the game.

Gordy decided that Michael could learn more from Diana. In October, 1969, at the age of eleven, he went to live with her for a month. She was like a second mother to him, taking him to museums and teaching him about art. When he wasn't working on his own music, Michael studied Diana. How did she sing? How did she dance? One day he watched her secretly as she looked in the mirror and practised.

In later years, Michael said that he had been a lonely child. When he lived with Diana Ross, he missed his real mother and often called her on the telephone. He was living the dream, but there was a price to pay.

'You can't do things that other children do,' he said, later, sadly. 'I didn't have friends when I was little. My brothers were my only friends.'

CHAPTER 2
'ABC, Easy as 1, 2, 3!'

London Heathrow airport, 1972. The Jackson 5 *were flying in from America to start a concert tour of twelve European cities. Their songs had been successful in Europe, but they didn't know what to expect at the airport. They certainly didn't expect thousands of screaming girls! Airport workers hadn't seen crowds like this since the days of the Beatles*. The fans raced towards the band, wanting to touch and kiss them. Jermaine lost some hair as girls fought to touch him. The screams were so loud that they brought tears to Marlon's eyes. It was worst for Michael. Several girls pulled on both ends of his scarf and almost killed him. It was the same everywhere – in Paris, Munich, Brussels, Amsterdam …* The Jackson 5 *had arrived!*

* The Beatles were a very popular British band in the 1960s. Their music is famous all over the world.

Life had changed for the Jackson boys, but how had this happened? The Jackson 5's first single for Motown Records was 'I Want You Back', in October 1969. It was not an immediate success, but Berry Gordy was confident about the band. Motown Records made sure that the single was often played on the radio and that record shops everywhere sold it. Soon the record became a number one hit in the United States. It was a hit in Britain, too, and in many other countries around the world.

In the same year, Michael's mother, sisters, and youngest brother, Randy, moved to Los Angeles, and the whole Jackson family lived together in a beautiful house in the hills above the city. For a while, Michael was a happy eleven year old again. 'I'm really excited about everything,' he said in an interview at the time.

Things got better and better. The band's first album, *Diana Ross Presents the Jackson 5*, appeared in December and was a huge success.

'Five brothers called Jackson who I discovered in Gary, Indiana,' wrote Diana Ross inside the album cover. 'They've got great talent.'

Of course, Diana Ross didn't really 'discover' the Jacksons – but it made a better story for the press.

Motown moved fast. The second Jackson 5 album, *ABC*, appeared early in 1970. Fans loved the title song and made it the band's second number-one single. This was quickly followed by 'The Love You Save', the band's third single and third number one hit – Berry Gordy had been right. The Jackson 5 made two more albums that year, but their time was not only spent in the studio. They toured America, playing concerts to bigger and bigger crowds. All of the brothers were great performers, but Michael was special. He really came alive when he was on stage.

   This gave Berry Gordy an idea. He decided that Michael needed to record a song on his own. Joe Jackson liked this idea, and so the first Michael Jackson record was made. 'Got To Be There' was Michael Jackson's first solo love song and it became a big hit around the world. Michael was only thirteen years old. With all of this success, the Jackson family bought a large new house in LA. Life was very different now from the old days in Gary, Indiana.

   But did this new life make Michael happy? He was in a famous band, his family was together again and their money problems were in the past. But life wasn't all perfect. Michael loved performing, but he did not always like touring. His older brothers enjoyed the attention of all the girl fans, but Michael was often frightened by all the screams. After the success of 'Got To Be There', more and more of the screams were for him. Although his brothers made jokes about this, they knew Michael was the real star of The Jackson 5.

Life in their big new home wasn't always happy either. Michael had never had a normal life, and he was often lonely. He had a lot of pet animals, but no real friends except his brothers and sisters. Like many teenagers, he wasn't happy with his appearance. He had the usual

teenage problems with the skin on his face and he hated his nose. Katherine noticed a big change in him around this time. He seemed less happy and he spent even more time by himself. He didn't like to look at people during conversations.

In 1972, the Jacksons continued to make albums and tour. In the same year, Michael recorded his first solo album but he did not get his first number one record until he sang a song about a pet rat! It was recorded for a film called *Ben*. The subject of the film was close to Michael's heart. In the story, a lonely boy becomes the friend of an intelligent rat called Ben. Michael had several pet rats himself.

Now the Jackson family had two different music careers with Motown – the band's and Michael's solo work. But, after their early success, The Jackson 5's album sales started falling. Joe Jackson became more and more angry with Berry Gordy and the record company. He felt that they were no longer interested in his sons' new music.

Michael's third solo album didn't sell well and Joe decided that it was time for a change. One of the problems at Motown was that the band didn't have any control over their career. The Jackson 5 recorded 469 songs at Motown and they weren't allowed to write any of them. But the Jackson boys were ready to write and play their own music – and Michael knew this.

The shy sixteen-year-old star decided to telephone Berry Gordy. 'You and I need to talk,' he told the head of Motown.

When they met, Michael explained that he wanted to write and produce his own music. Gordy didn't promise anything. 'If it wasn't for me, the Jacksons would still be in Gary, Indiana,' he said.

Michael felt bad but he realised that he and his brothers

had no choice. Soon after this the Jacksons met and voted to leave Motown.

Joe Jackson went to the big record company, CBS, who immediately offered him almost ten times the band's money from Motown. They also agreed to give the band more control over the music. It was hard to refuse an offer like this, but there was a problem. Two years earlier, Jermaine had married Berry Gordy's daughter, Hazel, and he did not want to leave Motown. He refused to sign the CBS papers. He wouldn't listen to his father or his brothers, and finally, minutes before a concert, he made his choice. Hazel and Motown had become more important than his father's plans for The Jackson 5. He left with his wife and the band performed without him.

A few months later, in March 1976, the Jackson four were five again. Jackie, Tito, Marlon, Michael and their youngest brother, Randy, joined CBS under the new name The Jackson Family. A bright new future lay before them.

CHAPTER 3
MEETING QUINCY JONES

It was another hot day in the city of New York. Michael Jackson was practising for his part in a new film called The Wiz. *Michael felt a little nervous. There was a word that he didn't know how to say. It was the name of a famous Greek thinker called 'Socrates'*. He tried to say it. The film's music producer, Quincy Jones, was watching.*

* Socrates ['sɒkrətiz] lived from 469 BC to 399 BC in Ancient Greece. He had many important thoughts and ideas about life.

*'Hey, Michael,' he called out. 'It's '**Soc**-ra-tes', not 'Soc-**rate**-es!'*
Michael's eyes were wide. 'Really?'

Michael liked Quincy and the work that he had done with other musicians. In fact, he had asked him if he could find him a good producer for his next album.

Now, Quincy smiled at the young star. It was clear that Michael was very talented. He knew everyone's songs, dance moves and words in the film. Quickly, Quincy decided something.

'I'll be your next producer!' he said.

In the summer of 1977, a group of writers and producers began an exciting new film project. They wanted to use the story of one of America's most popular films – *The Wizard of Oz* – to make a new African-American film – *The Wiz.* It would have some of America's top African-American singers. Diana Ross was chosen as Dorothy, and Michael Jackson was asked to play the part of the Scarecrow. Michael was very excited. He was going to be in the movies!

Michael moved to New York City to make the film. For the first time in his life, he could escape from his family and the recording studio. Working on *The Wiz* was hard at times – but Michael loved it. He also met the man who would change his musical career for ever – Quincy Jones.

When filming had finished, Michael returned to Los Angeles to work on the next album with his brothers. The band were now called The Jacksons. The brothers wrote almost all of the songs and produced the *Destiny* album themselves and it sounded great. At the same time, *The Wiz* came out – and this was not such a success. Fans didn't like it, and it made very litte money.

Michael felt he was ready to do more solo work, away from his father and the band. He called Quincy Jones and they agreed to work together on a new album – *Off The Wall*. However, Michael's record company were not happy about this. Quincy had begun his long career in the world of jazz music and they didn't think that he could produce a pop album. But together the young singer and the music producer were a perfect team.

Quincy remembers that Michael was very shy. 'He used to sing with his back to me, while I sat with my hands over

my eyes and the lights out,' he said.

Quincy encouraged Michael to record songs with more meaning – songs about love and feelings. 'We're not going to sing about pet rats anymore,' he joked.

Although he was now twenty years old, Michael had never really had a proper girlfriend. However, for a short time he was close friends with the young child actor, Tatum O'Neal. Michael recorded a slow, sad song about lost love called 'She's Out Of My Life'. He wrote this about Tatum, and the first time that he sang it in the studio, he cried at the end. They recorded it several times, but each time he cried. Finally, Quincy decided to leave the sound of Michael Jackson's tears on the song.

Everything about *Off The Wall* was fresh and new. With Quincy's help, Michael was trying new exciting things with his voice. He wrote three of the songs on the album, including the first single 'Don't Stop 'Til You Get Enough'. He had discovered that he could write songs for the album himself and help to shape the music. This was very different from his days at Motown.

The photo on the front of the album showed a new side of Michael, too. The sweet kid from The Jacksons had gone and a good-looking young man was in his place. In the photo he wore a black dinner suit. He also wore a pair of bright white socks – those were Michael's idea and they soon became a famous part of his new look.

The album came out in 1979, and it was a big hit. More than eight million copies of the album were sold around the world. Michael Jackson was back on top!

Since he was a teenager, Michael had always been unhappy with his nose. It was wide and flat, like his father's, and his brothers used to laugh at him. One day, he was practising dance moves for an *Off The Wall* concert tour, and he fell and broke his nose. For Michael, this accident was the perfect excuse. He flew back to LA and had plastic surgery for the first time. And when Michael Jackson saw his new nose, he liked what he saw . . . .

After the success of *Off The Wall*, Michael went on tour with The Jacksons but he wasn't really interested in the band anymore. He and Quincy started planning the next album. When they started to record in the studio, Quincy knew that this was something really special. All of Michael's talents were coming together for this unusual album. Its name? *Thriller*.

CHAPTER 4
THRILLER AND THE 'MOONWALK'

A car stops by the side of a dark road. The young man inside tells his girlfriend that it needs petrol. As they walk along the road together, he turns to her and says, 'You know, I'm not like other guys. I'm … different.'

His girfriend smiles. 'I know. That's why I like you.'

As the full moon appears from behind a cloud, the young man begins to change. His teeth get longer and hair grows all over his face. The girl can't stop screaming. Her night out with her new boyfriend has become a nightmare. Her screams ring through the clear night, as she runs into the woods.

In the early 1980s, the music world was changing. With the start of MTV* on television, fans expected more than just

* MTV is short for Music TV. It started in the 1980s and shows music videos.

a band performing their songs. But nothing prepared them for Michael Jackson's *Thriller* video. This wasn't just another video to sell a pop song - it was a 14-minute scary movie, with music and dancing! It was so popular that for a while MTV showed it twice every hour.

In fact, it was soon clear that the album *Thriller* was amazing in lots of ways. Again, Michael had written several songs himself – 'The Girl Is Mine' (sung with Paul McCartney*), 'Wanna Be Startin' Somethin'', 'Beat It', and 'Billie Jean'. As on the last album, there was a mix of musical styles; there was pop, soul and funk.

'Billie Jean' is about a girl who says that the singer is the father of her child. The idea came from real life. In the days of The Jackson 5, lots of girls used to say that one of the Jackson brothers was the father of their newborn children. 'I could never understand how these girls could say these things,' Michael said.

The making of *Thriller* wasn't always smooth. When the songs were first played back in the studio to Michael, he was very unhappy. He and Quincy had to mix all of the songs again. Michael thought the album sounded fantastic now, but there were still problems.

'This album won't sell as well as *Off The Wall*, Mike,' Quincy said. 'Record sales aren't good anywhere, at the moment.'

Michael couldn't believe it. If his producer didn't believe in *Thriller*, then he, Michael, didn't want to sell it. The head of the record company called him, and later, Michael chose to bring out the album, as they had planned. Of course, Michael was right. The album came out in December, 1981, and it was an immediate hit. It stayed in the US chart for over two years and went on to become the biggest-selling album ever: it has

* Paul McCartney is a famous UK singer. He used to be one of the lead singers in The Beatles.

sold over 100 million copies around the world.

The *Thriller* video played a big part in the album's success. Michael asked a horror film director to make the video with him. At a time when a good video could cost around $25,000, the *Thriller* video cost an amazing $600,000 to make. It suited the song's scary words perfectly, but for a while the video itself was in danger. Michael's church leaders decided that a song and video about dead people who come to life (and then dance!) did not send a good message. Michael wasn't sure if they should show it, after all. In the end, it played on TV with a message at the start, saying that the singer did not believe in the song's subject.

With *Thriller* out in record shops, Michael was no longer a star – he was a superstar. And he had more amazing surprises for his millions of fans. In 1983, Motown Records was twenty-five years old, and there were plans for a celebration on TV. Michael didn't want to appear in the show, but his brothers did. After long talks with the programme makers, Michael agreed to appear, if he had control of his performance.

On the night of the show, Michael was nervous, but when he walked out on stage, he looked confident. Viewers noticed that he was thinner and his nose looked different again. (He had had more plastic surgery.) He wore a black suit and hat, with white socks and one white glove. After singing a song with his brothers, Michael stayed on stage. The first notes of 'Billie Jean' started playing, and Michael threw his hat across the stage. Already, the crowd were going wild. And then he started to dance. His feet were going back but it seemed that he was moving forward at the same time. This amazing dance was called the 'moonwalk'– a brilliant mix of street dance and much older dance moves. People couldn't believe it; many thought that it was a trick with mirrors or cameras.

Michael Jackson performing
at the Motown TV show

Soon everyone was talking about Michael Jackson's
moonwalk, and teenagers around the world started doing
the dance on the street and in nightclubs. Around this time,
the US news magazine *Time* said: 'Jackson is the biggest thing
since The Beatles. He is the hottest solo act since Elvis. He
could be the most popular black singer ever.'

1984 was a great year for Michael. He won eight awards
at the Grammys, America's biggest music awards. He was
given a star on the Hollywood Walk of Fame*. And he was
even given a special award by US President Ronald Reagan
at the White House.

* The Walk of Fame on Hollywood Boulevard has pink stars on the
ground with the names of famous people inside them.

Things were not going as well for Michael's brothers. They wanted to make some money by touring again, as The Jacksons, and they needed Michael to join them. At first, Michael wasn't interested, but in the end, he agreed to appear with the family band again. The drinks company Pepsi-Cola were paying for the tour, and The Jacksons agreed to make two adverts for them. Michael wrote new words to the song of 'Billie Jean' for The Jacksons to perform.

'I don't have a good feeling about this,' Michael said at the time. Again, he didn't want to do the adverts, but he was only one voice against four others. In fact, Michael's 'feeling' was right. During the filming of the Pepsi advert, Michael was hurt.

MICHAEL JACKSON ON FIRE!

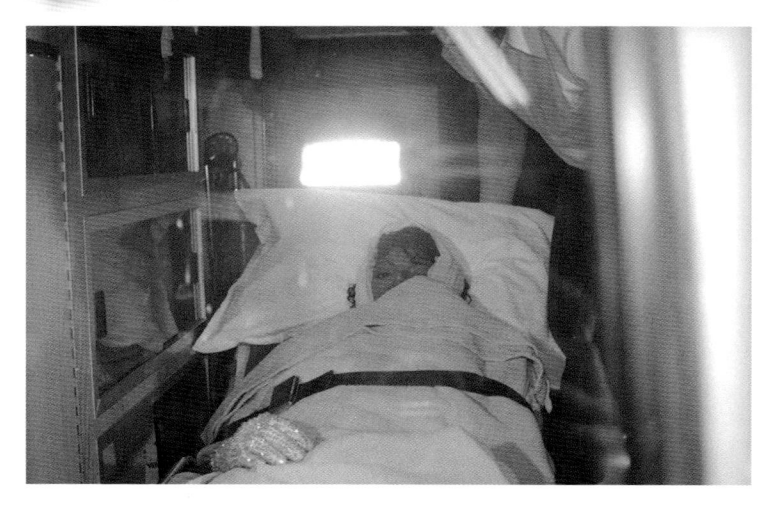

It didn't seem possible. Michael Jackson was on the front page of almost every newspaper, with his hair on fire! But it was true. During the filming of one of the Pepsi adverts, Michael's hair caught fire, in front of thousands of fans. He was quickly taken to a hospital in LA, still wearing his white glove, with a small burn on the back of his head. The story became big news when Michael's manager gave newspapers the photo. Fans all around the world couldn't believe it. It looked terrible … and terrible for Pepsi.

Pepsi did not want to be the company that hurt the biggest singer in the world; they gave Michael one and a half million dollars for the accident. Michael gave this money to the hospital where he had stayed. While Michael was in hospital with his injury, he was given medicine for the pain. This type of medicine later became a serious problem in his life.

Michael knew that soon he must make a new album. Finally, in 1986 – four years after *Thriller* came out – Michael was ready to try and answer the growing question: what can you do to follow the most successful album in history?

CHAPTER 5
'WACKO JACKO'

The photo in the newspaper was certainly strange. It showed Michael Jackson sleeping in a special machine, filled with oxygen. The story with the photo was even stranger: it said that Michael slept in this machine because he wanted to live longer. Michael's fans knew that the singer was never ordinary, but stories about him in the press were becoming more and more unusual. What was happening to Michael Jackson?

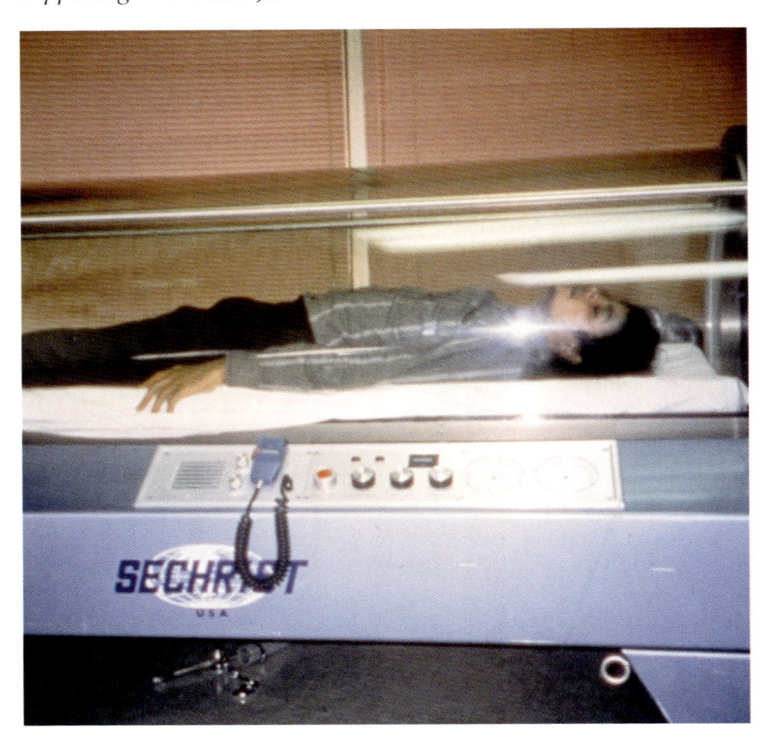

The strange photo first appeared in a US paper and quickly spread all over the world. Michael Jackson had first seen the oxygen machine in the hospital where he stayed after the Pepsi accident. He had become very interested in it and at the time he had said, 'If I get into this machine, I can live to be 150? I'll do it!'

However, one of the machines was never brought to Jackson's home. Many people think that the photo of him was just a joke – a way of controlling the press. At that time, Michael had made a short sci-fi film called *Captain EO*. Perhaps he hoped that the strange photo would advertise the film.

Soon everyone was talking about the oxygen machine, but there were stranger stories to come. A few weeks later, newspapers reported that Michael wanted to buy the skeleton of John Merrick from a hospital in London. When he was a child in the 1800s, Merrick had had a terrible illness which changed his appearance. People paid to see him at funfairs and he led a very sad life. Again, the story appeared all around the world: Michael Jackson was acting strangely again! However, the hospital told reporters that the story was not true; nobody had tried to buy Merrick's body. This led to the same question: were Michael and his managers playing games with the press?

Perhaps there was some truth in this, but it was soon clear that nobody could control all the stories about the singer. The British newspapers' new name for the singer was 'Wacko* Jacko', and stories about 'Wacko Jacko' sold newspapers. Some of these stories were true – there were many unusual things about Michael's life – but a lot of them were not. People loved to read about the singer's pet chimpanzee, Bubbles. In one story, the chimpanzee was Michael's best friend; in another, Michael was trying to speak

* 'wacko' means crazy.

animal language to his 'friend'. A chimpanzee may not be an ordinary pet, but Michael kept many unusual animals; most of the strange stories about Bubbles just weren't true.

WACKO JACKO: BLACK OR WHITE?

During the mid 1980s, Michael Jackson's appearance began to change. Lots of newspapers showed older photos of Michael as a teenager to show how his face had changed. Some doctors think that he had surgery ten times or more on his face. The most unusual thing about his appearance was the colour of his skin. Both of his parents were African-American, but clearly his skin was becoming much lighter. Michael said that he had an illness that made dark skin lighter. But many people thought that he was paying doctors to change his skin.

In July 1987, Michael's third album *Bad* came out. Music fans all around the world were excited, and the album sold well. *Rolling Stone* music magazine said it was 'richer and better' than *Thriller*. On the album cover, Michael Jackson

stands unsmiling in a black leather jacket. Michael's manager wanted people to see the singer differently – here was a new 'cool' Michael Jackson.

As with *Thriller*, Michael wanted the videos for *Bad* to be special. The video for the title song was made by famous movie director Martin

Scorsese. In the video, a young man fights back on the rough streets of a big city. Although it cost almost two million dollars to make, many people laughed at it and joked about Michael Jackson trying to look 'mean'.

MICHAEL JACKSON: HE'S BLACK, HE'S BAD – IS THIS GUY STRANGE, OR WHAT?

As the singer started his *Bad* tour of Japan in 1987, a US magazine wrote about him, saying that the singer had become really strange. It said that many people no longer understood Michael and so his music did not reach them in the same way. Michael was so upset that he wrote a letter to the magazine. 'I cry very often because it hurts, and I worry about the children,' he wrote.

It was a bad idea: the magazine printed the letter (with all of its spelling mistakes) and Michael seemed even stranger.

The news stories didn't stop. One said that he was in love with Princess Diana*; another said that he tried to speak to the ghost of Elvis Presley. To Michael, it seemed that they would never end.

* Princess Diana was the wife of Prince Charles in the UK from 1981 until 1996. She died in a car crash in Paris in 1997.

CHAPTER 6
NEVERLAND

At the entrance there were huge golden gates. Behind them, there was a fair with rides and lots of unusual animals. Music from Disney films played across the gardens. And there were lots of statues of Peter Pan – the boy from the famous story who stays a child forever in a place called Neverland. Michael thought his new home was perfect. 'I wanted a place where I could have everything that I never had as a child,' he said.

In July 1988, Michael decided to buy his own house. Even after his solo success, he still lived in his parents' house for much of the time. He bought a large Californian house, with a lot of land, and it cost around seventeen million dollars.

Michael called his new home 'Neverland'. Neverland is a place in the famous children's book, *Peter Pan*. For years, Michael had loved this story, and he started to make Neverland into a children's dream home.

Michael often invited groups of sick children to come to Neverland and enjoy all the rides and games. On tour, he always gave concert tickets to children who could not afford to go. In an interview, he said that the company of children helped him in his work.

'When I am with them, the music comes to me easily,' he said. 'When I'm tired or bored, children make me feel better.'

In 1991, Michael Jackson made his next album, *Dangerous*. This was with a new record company, Sony, and Michael made lots of money from it. To introduce the new album, there were parties all around the world. *Dangerous* sold millions of copies, and 'Black Or White' was a number one hit in the UK and the US.

One hot spring afternoon in 1992, Michael was driving through Beverly Hills, when his car stopped running. He stood by the side of the road and called 911* but they told him to call a garage, not the police. What was he going to do? Just then a man drove past and saw the famous singer. He couldn't believe it. He stopped and offered to help him. He called his friend, Dave Schwartz, who worked in a nearby garage. Schwartz's wife's son, Jordie, was a huge Michael Jackson fan. Straight away Dave telephoned his wife.

'Bring Jordie to the garage,' he said. 'There's a surprise here for him!'

Michael Jackson with Jordie and his mother and younger sister

Michael met twelve-year-old Jordie Chandler and his mother, and took Jordie's telephone number. He promised that he would call him, and he did. They quickly became friends, and a few weeks later, Jordie, his mother and sister came and stayed at Neverland for a while. Michael took them on a trip to Las Vegas, bought them expensive presents and often spoke to Jordie on the phone when they weren't together.

Many people thought that Michael shared so many interests with children because he had 'lost' these years himself. He was sometimes called a 'man-child'. It was certainly unusual for an adult pop star to want to be friends

* In the US, you call '911' if you need the police quickly.

with children, but most people believed that there were no darker reasons. However, Jordie's real father, Evan Chandler, was not happy that his son was spending so much time with Michael Jackson. He learnt from his wife that Michael and Jordie sometimes slept in the same room, when the family visited Neverland. In his opinion, something was very wrong.

Evan told Michael that he wanted twenty million dollars from him. If the singer didn't give him the money, Evan would call the police and tell them all about his worries. Many people have questioned Chandler's actions here. Why didn't he just go to the police? Money clearly played a big part. Michael refused, and so Evan Chandler called the police. While Michael was in Bangkok for the start of his *Dangerous* tour, the police were at Neverland, looking carefully at all of the singer's things.

Suddenly, the singer was in serious trouble. His mother Katherine wanted to help, but Michael did not want his parents around now. Instead Michael turned to his friend Elizabeth Taylor* for help. She helped to get the singer's team of lawyers together. While he was on the *Dangerous* tour, she passed on information to him.

It was a terrible time for Michael Jackson. When he returned to California, there were police everywhere in Neverland. The police planned to go through all of his bank information. This was all too much for the singer. He just wanted his life back. Michael decided to give the money to Evan Chandler and his son. As soon as he did, the police left Michael alone. Michael never saw Jordie again.

Michael Jackson was extremely upset about everything that had happened. 'I have never and would never hurt a child,' he said at the time.

* Elizabeth Taylor is a famous British film star.

In 1993, Michael invited the host of the US's most famous talk show, Oprah Winfrey, to Neverland. He hoped to show the real person behind the newspaper stories.

Michael gave Oprah a tour of Neverland and spoke about his early years in The Jackson 5. He said that he had had fun with his brothers, but that he had also been a lonely child.

'I remember going to the record studio and there was a park across the street. I saw all the children playing and I cried because I had to work instead,' he said.

He spoke, too, about all the Michael Jackson stories in the press. 'Someone writes a story about you and everybody believes it. If you hear something often enough, you start to believe it although it may not be true.'

It was Michael's first interview in fourteen years and it was watched by millions on television. He was still very popular with his fans, but the 'Wacko Jacko' stories in the press didn't stop. And sadly, there were still worse times ahead for the 'man child' singer.

CHAPTER 7
WIVES AND CHILDREN

In a hotel room in Bangkok, Michael Jackson picked up the telephone. He wanted to speak to his new girlfriend, Lisa Marie Presley. She was the only person who seemed to understand him, during these difficult times. She didn't care about the stories in the press. She was calm and gave him good advice. Lisa answered the phone, and straight away, Michael felt better. After a few minutes he said, 'If I asked you to marry me, would you do it?'

He didn't have to wait long for an answer.

'I would do it,' came the reply.

Lisa Marie Presley was the daughter of one of the most famous singers ever, Elvis Presley. She had first met Michael when she was six years old, and he was sixteen. They met again now in 1993 and they soon became close. Michael was having a difficult time. There was the fight with Evan Chandler, and he had health problems. He was addicted to painkillers. Lisa Marie had had similar problems and wanted to help him.

Michael and Lisa Marie also had similar pasts. Both had been famous children; both felt that they had 'missed' a normal life. The two of them talked on the phone almost every day. Although he was now 35 years old, Michael hadn't had many girlfriends, and some people were surprised that he and Lisa Marie were together. However in an interview at the time, Lisa Marie said, 'I like strange guys, the ones with fire . . . . That is Michael to me.'

So, in May, 1994, Michael and Lisa Marie were married in secret in the Dominican Republic. They didn't want the press to hear about it and their families knew nothing about it either. Lisa Marie's mother, Priscilla, was surprised. She thought Michael was only marrying her daughter because of her famous father, Elvis. Michael later said that he was sad that it wasn't a big wedding like his brother Jermaine's, and he was sorry that his mother wasn't there.

In fact, after the wedding, Lisa Marie never moved into Neverland. Her house was about two hours away. She already had two children with her first husband. She and her children often came to stay with Michael for a few days, but they always went back home. It seemed strange, but people around the couple said that it was love.

Michael and Lisa Marie showed this love to 250 million viewers of the MTV Music Awards in September, 1994. It was their first TV appearance together. Before they went on stage, Michael said to his new wife, 'I'm going to kiss you when we're up there.'

'No, you're not,' Lisa Marie told him. 'I don't want to.'

But she had learned one thing: if Michael wanted to do something, he did it. The world watched as Michael kissed her on stage – a kiss that didn't seem very natural … .

Soon there were problems between the couple. Perhaps the biggest problem was that Michael wanted to have children of their own. Lisa Marie wasn't so sure; she wanted to wait.

Michael and Janet Jackson
in the 'Scream' video.

In one fight, Michael joked that he knew a woman ready to have his children. He was talking about a nurse called Debbie Rowe. Lisa Marie laughed and said, 'Go ahead!'

Married life for the couple reached an end quickly. After nineteen months together, Lisa Marie left Michael. Years later, she said, 'We were two unusual people who did not know a 'normal life'. However, I believe he loved me as much as he could. And I loved him very much.'

While the couple were still married, Michael made another album called *HIStory*. It was a double album that contained his greatest hits and a new song called 'Scream'. Michael sang this song with his sister, Janet. Janet Jackson was now a big star too and had had several hit albums. The video for 'Scream' was the most expensive ever made at the time. 'Scream' was Michael's message to all the reporters who wrote untrue stories about him in their papers.

⭐ ⭐ ⭐

I'M HAVING MICHAEL JACKSON'S BABY!

It soon became clear that Michael's words to Lisa Marie about Debbie Rowe were not a joke. The nurse was going to have his baby! When Katherine Jackson found out, she wanted the two to marry. Michael agreed that this was a good idea, and so on November 15th, 1996, he married Debbie. Love played no part in this arrangement.

A baby boy arrived in February, 1997. He was given the name Prince Michael I. Michael took the baby back to

Michael Jackson and his wife, Debbie Rowe, 1997

Neverland, while Debbie continued to live in her own house. She didn't see much of the baby, but in April, 1998, she had a second child with Michael. This time it was a girl – Paris Katherine Michael Jackson. After this birth, Debbie learned that she probably could not have more children. By 1999, she and Michael were no longer married, and she played no real part in the children's lives after that.

Now a father of two, Michael worked on his next album, *Invincible*. Nobody knew it at the time, but this would be his final studio album. It sold more than eight million copies around the world, but times had changed: Michael no longer seemed to be at the centre of the music world.

⭐ ⭐ ⭐

JACKO HANGS BABY SON FROM HOTEL WINDOW!

In 2002, Michael had one more child – another son, Prince Michael II. Nobody knew who the mother was. The baby was also known by the rather strange name of Blanket*! Soon after he was born, Blanket became a big story in newspapers around the world when Michael was staying in a hotel in Berlin. Michael came to the window and held the baby out high over the crowd of fans outside. People around the

* A 'blanket' is a warm bedcover made of wool.

world were angry and surprised; they said that this was a dangerous and stupid thing to do. Michael quickly said sorry. 'It was a terrible mistake,' he said.

At the time, many people attacked the singer, saying that he was not a good parent. But as one of the most famous people in the world, Michael was afraid for his children's safety. When they went outside, their faces were often covered because Michael didn't want people to see them. Unlike some other stars, he never wanted his children in photos with him. He had never had a chance to be a child and he didn't want this to be true for his own children.

CHAPTER 8
Hard times

Everyone was excited when the video arrived. Michael and his team all sat excitedly around the TV. After five minutes the feeling in the room was very different. This interview had been a terrible mistake. Everyone started talking at once – what should they do next? Michael just shook his head and said, 'I can't believe that he could do this to me.'

It was 2003 and Michael wanted to be back on top. He had always loved Princess Diana and he remembered her TV interview with British reporter Martin Bashir. After so many untrue stories about her in the press, people enjoyed hearing Diana speak about her life. Many people felt sorry for her, and she became extremely popular.

Michael decided that he needed the same. He said that Bashir could come to Neverland and film him over almost eight months. For once, Michael did not have total control. If he didn't like something in Bashir's film, he could not change or cut it. But Michael was confident that he could show the world the true Michael Jackson.

When people saw Bashir's film *Living with Michael Jackson* on television, they were surprised to learn that Michael was still inviting children out to Neverland. Sometimes they stayed at the house and sometimes Michael and these boys slept in the same room. In the interview, Michael spoke openly about this. 'We read a story, we drink hot milk – it's very natural, very sweet,' he said.

 But not everyone saw things in the same way as Michael. He even put out his own TV interview, trying to explain the

Bashir film. But this wasn't so easy. One of the children at Neverland during the making of the film was Gavin Arvizo. He was at Neverland because he had been very sick. After the Bashir film was shown, the LA police received a phone call from a doctor. She had seen the film and thought that there was something wrong with Michael and Gavin's friendship. She suggested that maybe Michael was breaking the law.

The police went and interviewed the Arvizo family. At first they said that Michael had helped their son get better. But they soon changed this story, saying that there had been a crime. It was quickly becoming a nightmare for Michael. In yet another TV interview, he was asked about Gavin Arvizo.

'I've helped many, many, many children,' he answered. 'Thousands of children, sick kids. This is one of many.'

In November, 2003, the police went to Neverland and searched the house once again. This time they arrested Michael Jackson. The nightmare was getting worse and worse.

In 2005, he was taken to court. This was one of the hardest times of his life. He did not have to come to court often, but when he did he looked weak and ill. He was sleeping badly and he wasn't eating well. It seemed that he was taking more and more painkillers to help him through this difficult time. A few times he arrived at the court in his bed clothes. Michael never changed his story. 'I will say again that I have never, and would never, hurt a child,' he said.

More was learned about the Arvizo family. Years ago they had almost taken a big department store to court, saying that the store police had hurt their children. In the end, the store gave the family money because they didn't want to go to court. Was the same thing happening again?

After four long months in court, it was agreed that Michael had done nothing wrong. He was free to go. For Michael, life would never be the same again. His manager at the time later said, 'The Bashir programme broke him. It killed him. He took a long time to die, but it started that night.'

Michael Jackson and his father (far right) going to court, 2005

JACKO'S WACKO NEVERLAND SALE!

Neverland was in trouble. After the recent police searches, the place no longer felt like home for Michael. He also had serious money problems. More than forty people worked at Neverland and the house alone cost Michael five million dollars a year. In the spring of 2006, Neverland closed. Plans were made to sell the unusual collection of Michael's things. Ten trucks were filled with clothes, games, pianos, statues, and lots of books and photographs. Fans became very excited when they heard about the sale. But the sale never happened. A few months later, Michael decided against it. All of his things at Neverland were just too important to him.

Michael's money problems had not gone away. Of course, he was still earning lots of money; he was just spending even more! When he visited a hotel, he paid for the best and usually took around twenty people with him. Some people say that in one year Michael spent twenty-five million dollars more than he earned.

Then Michael's big brother Jermaine had an idea. Jermaine had a friend in Bahrain, Sheikh* Abdullah. The sheikh was very rich, and he was very interested in pop music. He wanted to make music with Michael Jackson. Michael flew to Bahrain in 2005 with his children, and the two men started making plans. The sheikh was building a studio there for Michael, and he wanted to start his own record company. He gave Michael seven million dollars.

* A *sheikh* is a leader in an Arab country.

However, after a few months, Michael left Bahrain, deciding that he didn't want to work with the sheikh. He started working on the *Thriller 25* album in Ireland. This was a new mix of his most famous album, now twenty-five years old. To celebrate this and make the album more modern, Michael worked with popular younger artists like Kanye West and Will.i.am from the band The Black Eyed Peas. *Thriller 25* came out in 2008.

In the same year, Michael was told that he had to go back to court, this time in London. Sheikh Abdullah was saying that the singer had to pay him back the seven million dollars. Michael said that he and the sheikh had never had a business agreement and that the money had been a gift. Just before Michael flew to England, he learned that his lawyers had reached an agreement with the sheikh's lawyers. He didn't have to go to court.

Neverland was sold now, but Michael still needed money. And so, four months later he made an important choice. Finally, after many years, the 'King of Pop' would perform again. He would play his last ever concerts in London. And he got on a plane to England to give the news to the world's press.

CHAPTER 9
'THIS IS IT!'

'London, welcome the King of Pop, Mr Michael Jackson!'
The crowds of fans screamed, as Michael Jackson appeared on stage, wearing a black and silver jacket and sunglasses. He smiled and waved at the crowd. 'This is it!' he said. 'These will be my final performances in London. This really is it. I love you. See you in July!'

It was true. Michael Jackson was going to perform again for the first time in twelve years. He was going to give fifty concerts in London from July 2009 to March 2010. All of the tickets were sold in just a few hours. Fans who weren't even born at the time of *Thriller* wanted to see him. And, of course, older fans wanted to watch him perform and see the moonwalk one more time.

In the months before his death, Michael was very busy. Dancers were chosen for the shows and he was practising hard with them. But Michael had not performed for a long time. He was fifty years old. Could he still sing and dance for two hours, night after night? A newspaper reported that Michael had told a group of fans in the US, 'I don't know how I'm going to do fifty shows. I only wanted to do ten.'

However, his record company believed that he was ready. Doctors said that his health was fine, but to the outside world, Michael often seemed too thin and weak. In fact, Michael was having terrible problems. He couldn't sleep at night and he had become addicted to a mix of very strong painkillers.

On the last day of his life, Michael was at his house in LA. He had slept very badly, and he asked his private doctor, Dr Conrad Murray, to give him a very strong painkiller called 'propofol'*. Dr Murray agreed.

At around midday, Michael Jackson fell to the floor. Was it a heart attack? Dr Murray tried to help him while a guard called 911 for help. Michael was taken to hospital but doctors there were unable to save him. He died at 2.26 pm.

⭐ ⭐ ⭐

A SAD GOODBYE TO THE KING OF POP

On July 7th, 2009, the Jackson family held a service at a large theatre in LA to say goodbye to Michael. There were almost 18,000 free tickets for Michael's fans, but many more wanted to come. The celebration lasted over two hours and

* Propofol is usually given to patients before surgery.

was shown on TV all over the world. Michael's brothers carried his body on to the stage. Each brother was wearing one white glove, like Michael had done.

Many famous people spoke about Michael with love and sadness at his early death. Berry Gordy remembered the old days when The Jackson 5 were with Motown Records; he knew then that Michael was 'special'. Kind messages from Nelson Mandela*, Elizabeth Taylor, and Diana Ross were read out. Mariah Carey, Lionel Ritchie, Stevie Wonder and Usher all sang for the crowd. Jermaine Jackson sang one of Michael's favourites, 'Smile', an old Charlie Chaplin* song.

* Nelson Mandela was the first black president of South Africa.
* Charlie Chaplin made and acted in silent films. 'Smile' was the music for one of his last silent films in 1936.

Several people at the service spoke of how Michael had opened doors for African-Americans. More of his videos were shown on television than any other black singer before him; his face was on the cover of more magazines. In the song 'Black Or White', Michael had sung, 'It doesn't matter if you're black or white'. His own career helped to make this true.

Paris Jackson, Michael's eleven-year-old daughter, ended the service. With the Jackson family all around her, she spoke about her father. 'Daddy has been the best father that you could ever imagine,' she said.

After Michael's death, his music was everywhere again. The *Thriller* album and albums by The Jackson 5 were back in the top ten in the UK. And there was talk of new music, too. In the last years of his life, Michael had worked on songs for a new album.

Much of Michael Jackson's life will stay a mystery to the outside world. Why was he never able to enjoy a happy married life? Was he the real father of the three children, Prince Michael, Paris and Blanket? And why didn't his family and friends try to help with his dangerous addiction to painkillers?

Who was Michael Jackson? Many will remember him best for his music and amazing dance moves. Many families will remember his kindness to their sick children. Others will remember the strange stories in the press and the unusual way that he lived his life. One thing is certain – for forty years, Michael Jackson gave the world music and performances that people will remember for a long time. The 'King of Pop' may be dead but his music lives on.

MEMORIES OF MICHAEL

When the news of Michael Jackson's death on 26th June, 2009 reached fans around the world, thousands wrote about it on social networking sites such as Twitter and Facebook. He gave fans, young and old, some wonderful music, and was a strong musical influence on many singers and songwriters. How was the 'King of Pop' remembered?

President Barack Obama

'I often listened to Michael Jackson when I was a kid in Hawaii. He was one of our greatest performers.'

Justin Timberlake

In 2001, Justin Timberlake performed with Michael Jackson at the MTV Music Video Awards. 'I'm lucky to have memories with him on and off stage … . He really was, and always will, be the 'King of Pop.' '

Quincy Jones, producer on *Off The Wall, Thriller* and *Bad*

'I'm devastated. The music that we recorded in the '80s is played in every corner of the world. I've lost my little brother, and part of me has gone with him.'

Britney Spears

'I was so excited about seeing his tour in London, and performing with him there. I'm devastated.'

Beyoncé

'This is a terrible day. Michael Jackson will always be the King of Pop.'

Madonna

'I can't stop crying.'

Live Concerts

Many musicians were in the middle of concert tours when they heard the news. Madonna had a huge picture of Michael above the stage while his songs played. A dancer dressed like Michael and performed all of his famous dance moves, while Madonna watched. At the end she said, 'To one of the greatest artists that the world has ever known!'

P Diddy

'He made the music come alive. I will miss him.'

The Memorial Service, Los Angeles

Many stars performed and spoke about Michael at the memorial service in Los Angeles. People watched it live on TV all over the world.

Usher sang one of Michael's songs, 'Gone Too Soon', and started to cry during his song. 'My music wouldn't be the same without Michael Jackson. His death has been very, very hard for me.'

'*Sing our songs among the stars and walk our dances across the face of the moon …*'
Queen Latifah read a poem which was written about Michael by black writer Maya Angelou.

twitter
'Michael Jackson is now moonwalking in heaven. RIP.*'

twitter
'Thanks for the music and the memories. RIP, MJ.'

What do these words mean? You can use a dictionary.
social networking site   influence   memory
devastated   heaven   memorial service   poem

What memories do you have of Michael Jackson and his music? What will people remember most about him, do you think?

* We say 'Rest in Peace' (RIP) when someone dies.

BLACK OR WHITE?

MICHAEL JACKSON, MOTOWN AND THE COLOUR BARRIER

When Michael Jackson first started singing in the 1960s, the music business was very different in the US. There was the main pop chart, but there was also a chart for R&B (Rhythm and Blues) music. Most African-American artists had their music only on the R&B chart. Many radio stations only played music from one chart or the other. Michael Jackson's success helped to change this.

'WHITES, ONLY'

African-American artists had faced problems for years. Sammy Davis, Jr was a famous performer and singer. In 1945, he was paid a lot of money to perform at a big hotel in Las Vegas. There was just one problem: at first he was not allowed to stay in the hotel; it was for white people only.

THE MOTOWN YEARS

Stevie Wonder

In 1960, African-American Berry Gordy started a new record company – Motown. Gordy wanted to bring black music to white America. He carefully controlled the image of his artists – including their clothes and dance style. Gordy believed that this image would help white Americans to become more interested in music by African-American artists. It worked: Motown had many hugely successful black artists in the 1960s and '70s including Marvin Gaye, Diana Ross, Stevie Wonder and, of course, The Jackson 5 and Michael Jackson. Things had changed a lot, but many people still spoke about a 'colour barrier' for African-American artists.

Diana Ross with the Supremes

Michael Jackson's 'Thriller' video

MICHAEL AND MTV

In the early 1980s, the music channel MTV appeared. It was very popular with teenagers. At first, the channel played mostly rock music by white artists, but Michael Jackson's huge success changed all of this.

In 1983, Michael's record company CBS wanted MTV to play the 'Billie Jean' video. MTV refused, saying it was the wrong kind of music for the channel. CBS said that they would take all of their other artists away from MTV if they didn't play Michael Jackson's videos. The channel agreed to play 'Billie Jean' several times each day and it was hugely popular. The same was true for the 'Thriller' video, and many other Michael Jackson hits.

After Michael Jackson's solo success in the 1980s, it was less unusual for black singers to be on MTV, to be on the front cover of magazines, and to be in the main pop charts. Many African-American artists believe that Michael Jackson opened the door to a fairer world for them.

What do these words mean? You can use a dictionary.

barrier   chart   image   channel

What kind of music do you like? Do you know its history?

CHILD STARS:
TOO FAMOUS
TOO YOUNG?

Big Brother, X-Factor, Britain's Got Talent – with the growing number of TV 'talent' shows, it sometimes seems that everybody wants to be famous, and this includes children. But as Michael Jackson's story shows, becoming a child star doesn't always lead to a happy life. Young stars have to grow up very quickly. Is it possible to be too famous too young?

THE WORLD'S FIRST CHILD STAR

Shirley Temple was a huge movie star in the 1930s. She made her first movie at the age of five. She could act, sing and dance and her movies made a lot of money. However, Shirley Temple did not continue acting as an adult and her movie career ended when she was about 20. In later life, she worked as a politician.

FRIENDS OF MICHAEL

Michael Jackson felt close to people who had been child stars. One of his close friends was Elizabeth Taylor, the famous actress. Another friend was Macaulay Culkin. In 1990, when Macaulay was ten, he starred in the first of the *Home Alone* movies. However, his success came with family problems; his parents started to fight over divorce arrangements and money. Macaulay said that he wouldn't act again until they stopped fighting. It took two years for it to end. As an adult, Macaulay hasn't had any more hit movies.

BRITNEY SPEARS AND THE DISNEY 'STAR FACTORY'

Britney Spears was chosen to be on Disney's *All New Mickey Mouse Club* on television when she was ten years old. Justin Timberlake and Christina Aguilera were on the show at the same time! Six years later, she had a hit with '(Hit Me), Baby One More Time'. It was the start of a hugely successful career but Britney had many problems. In 1994 she married an old school friend in Las Vegas but ended the marriage after 55 hours. She had two children with her next husband, but that marriage also ended. At times she has seemed out of control, and she is often followed by a large group of press photographers.

TEENAGE MOVIE STARS

Actors in two of the world's biggest movies were child stars. **Kristen Stewart** plays Bella in the *Twilight* films. Her first big film was *Panic Room* with Jodie Foster, when she was twelve. Kristen wants to become a writer one day too.

Harry Potter star **Daniel Radcliffe** made his first television appearance when he was ten. Then he got the part of Harry Potter. As well as the Harry Potter films, Daniel has made other movies and appeared on stage in London and New York. 'I do everything that a normal teenager does,' he said in one interview. 'I'm very normal!'

What do these words mean? You can use a dictionary.

grow up   childhood   divorce   marriage

What are the biggest dangers for a child star, do you think?

61

CHAPTERS 1–3

Before you read

You can use your dictionary.

1 Complete the sentences with these words.

addicted (to) album award career control competition manager performance rat single solo surgery stage studio talented

a) Michael Jackson could sing and dance brilliantly. He was very … .

b) Every pop star or band needs a … to help them with their business.

c) At the Oscars, people from the film business are given … .

d) Pop stars usually record music in a … .

e) A group of songs by one artist is called an… .

f) The best song from an album is often the first … .

g) 'I don't know what to do when I leave school. Can you give me some … advice?'

h) She won the school music …. by singing a song.

i) People often need to stay in hospital for a few days after … .

j) A … can be a good pet.

k) Sometimes singers leave their bands and become … artists.

l) I live to see bands play on … .

m) The crowd at the concert loved the band. It was a great … .

n) He's … cigarettes. He smokes two packets every day.

o) 'My parents don't let me do anything. They … my life!'

2 Look at 'People and places' on pages 4–5. Answer these questions.

a) When was Michael Jackson born?

b) How many wives did he have?

c) What is his daughter's name?

d) Where was Michael Jackson born?

After you read

3 Are these sentences true or false? Correct the false sentences.

a) Michael Jackson was always a happy child.

b) Michael had lots of money in Gary, Indiana.

c) It was Jermaine Jackson's idea to start a band.

d) The first three singles for The Jackson 5 were big hits.

e) Berry Gordy wanted The Jackson 5 to write their songs.

f) Michael Jackson broke his nose in a car accident.

4 What do you think?
  a) What will happen to The Jacksons?
  b) Will Michael Jackson become happier as he gets more successful?

CHAPTERS 4–6

Before you read

5 Answer the questions with the correct words below.
  lawyer statue skeleton
  a) If you are in trouble with the police, what could you need?
  b) If you got to an art museum, what could you see?
  c) If you study to be a doctor, what must you learn the parts of?

6 Complete the sentences with these words.
  advert chimpanzee interview oxygen
  a) I saw an … on TV for a new chocolate bar.
  b) The president gave an … to several newspaper reporters.
  c) Everybody needs … to live.
  d) The zoo's … had a baby.

After you read

7 Put these events in the right order.
  a) The police searched Neverland.
  b) Motown celebrated 25 years.
  c) Michael made the album *Bad*.
  d) Oprah Winfrey interviewed Michael in Neverland.
  e) *Dangerous* sold millions of copies around the world.
  f) Pepsi paid for two adverts with The Jackson 5.
  g) Michael met Jordie Chandler.
  h) Michael started his *Bad* tour in Japan.

8 Match the sentence halves.
  a) *Thriller* sold …   i) … 'Neverland'.
  b) Michael called his house …   ii) … over 100 million copies.
  c) Pepsi gave Michael …   iii) … eight Grammy awards.
  d) In 1984 Michael won …   iv) … one and a half million dollars.
  e) Michael bought his first house… v) … for seventeen million dollars.

9 What do you think?

Why do newspapers write stories about stars that aren't true?

CHAPTERS 7–9

Before you read

10 Complete the sentences with the correct words.

arrest court service

a) 'The church …. on Sunday morning was beautiful.

b) The police are looking for the criminal. They want to … him.

c) It is decided in … if someone must go to prison or not.

11 Answer these questions

a) Why do you think children were so important to Michael Jackson?

b) Chapter 8 is called 'Hard times'. What hard times did Michael Jackson face in his last years, do you think?

After you read

12 Who said it and when? Match the names with the sentences and write the answers.

Lisa Marie Presley Michael Jackson Michael's manager Paris Jackson

a) 'I will say again that I have never, and would never, hurt a child.'

b) 'I like strange guys, the ones with fire.'

c) 'The Bashir programme broke him. It killed him.'

d) 'Daddy has been the best father that you could ever imagine.'

e) 'It was a terrible mistake.'

f) 'This is it!'

13 Where did these things happen?

a) Michael Jackson and Lisa Marie Presley's wedding

b) Michael and Lisa Marie's on stage kiss

c) Michael holding Blanket out of a window

d) Michael speaking to his fans about his final concerts

e) The service for Michael Jackson, after his death

14 What do you think?

a) Did Michael Jackson have a good life? Why or why not?

b) Would you like to be famous? Why or why not?